THIS BOOK BELONGS TO:

DAILY PLAN

TODAY'S SCHEDULE

6-7 AM	
7-8 AM	
8-9 AM	
9-10 AM	
10-11 AM	
11-12 AM	
12-1 PM	
1-2 PM	
2-3 PM	
3-4 PM	
4-5 PM	
6-7 PM	
7-8 PM	
8-9 PM	

TOP PRIORITIES

NOTE..

DAILY PLAN

TODAY'S SCHEDULE

| 6-7 AM |
| 7-8 AM |
| 8-9 AM |
| 9-10 AM |
| 10-11 AM |
| 11-12 AM |
| 12-1 PM |
| 1-2 PM |
| 2-3 PM |
| 3-4 PM |
| 4-5 PM |
| 6-7 PM |
| 7-8 PM |
| 8-9 PM |

DATE

TOP PRIORITIES

TO DO LIST..

FOR TOMORROW..

NOTE..

DAILY PLAN

TODAY'S SCHEDULE

6-7 AM	
7-8 AM	
8-9 AM	
9-10 AM	
10-11 AM	
11-12 AM	
12-1 PM	
1-2 PM	
2-3 PM	
3-4 PM	
4-5 PM	
6-7 PM	
7-8 PM	
8-9 PM	

TOP PRIORITIES

NOTE..

DAILY PLAN

TODAY'S SCHEDULE

6-7 AM	
7-8 AM	
8-9 AM	
9-10 AM	
10-11 AM	
11-12 AM	
12-1 PM	
1-2 PM	
2-3 PM	
3-4 PM	
4-5 PM	
6-7 PM	
7-8 PM	
8-9 PM	

TOP PRIORITIES

NOTE..

DAILY PLAN

TODAY'S SCHEDULE

Time	
6-7 AM	
7-8 AM	
8-9 AM	
9-10 AM	
10-11 AM	
11-12 AM	
12-1 PM	
1-2 PM	
2-3 PM	
3-4 PM	
4-5 PM	
6-7 PM	
7-8 PM	
8-9 PM	

TOP PRIORITIES

TO DO LIST..

FOR TOMORROW..

NOTE..

DAILY PLAN

TODAY'S SCHEDULE

Time	
6-7 AM	
7-8 AM	
8-9 AM	
9-10 AM	
10-11 AM	
11-12 AM	
12-1 PM	
1-2 PM	
2-3 PM	
3-4 PM	
4-5 PM	
6-7 PM	
7-8 PM	
8-9 PM	

TOP PRIORITIES

NOTE..

DAILY PLAN

TODAY'S SCHEDULE

Time	
6-7 AM	
7-8 AM	
8-9 AM	
9-10 AM	
10-11 AM	
11-12 AM	
12-1 PM	
1-2 PM	
2-3 PM	
3-4 PM	
4-5 PM	
6-7 PM	
7-8 PM	
8-9 PM	

TOP PRIORITIES

FOR TOMORROW..

NOTES..

DAILY PLAN

TODAY'S SCHEDULE

6-7 AM	
7-8 AM	
8-9 AM	
9-10 AM	
10-11 AM	
11-12 AM	
12-1 PM	
1-2 PM	
2-3 PM	
3-4 PM	
4-5 PM	
6-7 PM	
7-8 PM	
8-9 PM	

TOP PRIORITIES

TO DO LIST..

FOR TOMORROW..

NOTE..

DAILY PLAN

DATE

TODAY'S SCHEDULE

6-7 AM	
7-8 AM	
8-9 AM	
9-10 AM	
10-11 AM	
11-12 AM	
12-1 PM	
1-2 PM	
2-3 PM	
3-4 PM	
4-5 PM	
6-7 PM	
7-8 PM	
8-9 PM	

TOP PRIORITIES

TO DO LIST..

FOR TOMORROW..

NOTE..

DAILY PLAN

TODAY'S SCHEDULE

6-7 AM	
7-8 AM	
8-9 AM	
9-10 AM	
10-11 AM	
11-12 AM	
12-1 PM	
1-2 PM	
2-3 PM	
3-4 PM	
4-5 PM	
6-7 PM	
7-8 PM	
8-9 PM	

TOP PRIORITIES

NOTE..

DAILY PLAN

DATE

TODAY'S SCHEDULE

6-7 AM	
7-8 AM	
8-9 AM	
9-10 AM	
10-11 AM	
11-12 AM	
12-1 PM	
1-2 PM	
2-3 PM	
3-4 PM	
4-5 PM	
6-7 PM	
7-8 PM	
8-9 PM	

TOP PRIORITIES

TO DO LIST..

FOR TOMORROW..

NOTE..

DAILY PLAN

DATE

TODAY'S SCHEDULE

6-7 AM	
7-8 AM	
8-9 AM	
9-10 AM	
10-11 AM	
11-12 AM	
12-1 PM	
1-2 PM	
2-3 PM	
3-4 PM	
4-5 PM	
6-7 PM	
7-8 PM	
8-9 PM	

TOP PRIORITIES

TO DO LIST..

FOR TOMORROW..

NOTE..

DAILY PLAN

TODAY'S SCHEDULE

Time	
6-7 AM	
7-8 AM	
8-9 AM	
9-10 AM	
10-11 AM	
11-12 AM	
12-1 PM	
1-2 PM	
2-3 PM	
3-4 PM	
4-5 PM	
6-7 PM	
7-8 PM	
8-9 PM	

TOP PRIORITIES

TO DO LIST..

FOR TOMORROW..

NOTE..

DAILY PLAN

TODAY'S SCHEDULE

6-7 AM

7-8 AM

8-9 AM

9-10 AM

10-11 AM

11-12 AM

12-1 PM

1-2 PM

2-3 PM

3-4 PM

4-5 PM

6-7 PM

7-8 PM

8-9 PM

TOP PRIORITIES

TO DO LIST..

FOR TOMORROW..

NOTE..

DAILY PLAN

TODAY'S SCHEDULE

Time	
6-7 AM	
7-8 AM	
8-9 AM	
9-10 AM	
10-11 AM	
11-12 AM	
12-1 PM	
1-2 PM	
2-3 PM	
3-4 PM	
4-5 PM	
6-7 PM	
7-8 PM	
8-9 PM	

TOP PRIORITIES

NOTE..

DAILY PLAN

TODAY'S SCHEDULE

6-7 AM	
7-8 AM	
8-9 AM	
9-10 AM	
10-11 AM	
11-12 AM	
12-1 PM	
1-2 PM	
2-3 PM	
3-4 PM	
4-5 PM	
6-7 PM	
7-8 PM	
8-9 PM	

TOP PRIORITIES

NOTE..

DAILY PLAN

TODAY'S SCHEDULE

6-7 AM	
7-8 AM	
8-9 AM	
9-10 AM	
10-11 AM	
11-12 AM	
12-1 PM	
1-2 PM	
2-3 PM	
3-4 PM	
4-5 PM	
6-7 PM	
7-8 PM	
8-9 PM	

TOP PRIORITIES

NOTE..

DAILY PLAN

TODAY'S SCHEDULE

6-7 AM	
7-8 AM	
8-9 AM	
9-10 AM	
10-11 AM	
11-12 AM	
12-1 PM	
1-2 PM	
2-3 PM	
3-4 PM	
4-5 PM	
6-7 PM	
7-8 PM	
8-9 PM	

TOP PRIORITIES

NOTE..

DAILY PLAN

TODAY'S SCHEDULE

6-7 AM	
7-8 AM	
8-9 AM	
9-10 AM	
10-11 AM	
11-12 AM	
12-1 PM	
1-2 PM	
2-3 PM	
3-4 PM	
4-5 PM	
6-7 PM	
7-8 PM	
8-9 PM	

TOP PRIORITIES

NOTE..

DAILY PLAN

TODAY'S SCHEDULE

6-7 AM	
7-8 AM	
8-9 AM	
9-10 AM	
10-11 AM	
11-12 AM	
12-1 PM	
1-2 PM	
2-3 PM	
3-4 PM	
4-5 PM	
6-7 PM	
7-8 PM	
8-9 PM	

TOP PRIORITIES

NOTE..

DAILY PLAN

TODAY'S SCHEDULE

6-7 AM	
7-8 AM	
8-9 AM	
9-10 AM	
10-11 AM	
11-12 AM	
12-1 PM	
1-2 PM	
2-3 PM	
3-4 PM	
4-5 PM	
6-7 PM	
7-8 PM	
8-9 PM	

TOP PRIORITIES

FOR TOMORROW..

NOTE..

DAILY PLAN

TODAY'S SCHEDULE

Time	
6-7 AM	
7-8 AM	
8-9 AM	
9-10 AM	
10-11 AM	
11-12 AM	
12-1 PM	
1-2 PM	
2-3 PM	
3-4 PM	
4-5 PM	
6-7 PM	
7-8 PM	
8-9 PM	

TOP PRIORITIES

TO DO LIST..

FOR TOMORROW..

NOTE..

DAILY PLAN

DATE

TODAY'S SCHEDULE

6-7 AM	
7-8 AM	
8-9 AM	
9-10 AM	
10-11 AM	
11-12 AM	
12-1 PM	
1-2 PM	
2-3 PM	
3-4 PM	
4-5 PM	
6-7 PM	
7-8 PM	
8-9 PM	

TOP PRIORITIES

TO DO LIST..

FOR TOMORROW..

NOTE..

DAILY PLAN

DATE

TODAY'S SCHEDULE

6-7 AM	
7-8 AM	
8-9 AM	
9-10 AM	
10-11 AM	
11-12 AM	
12-1 PM	
1-2 PM	
2-3 PM	
3-4 PM	
4-5 PM	
6-7 PM	
7-8 PM	
8-9 PM	

TOP PRIORITIES

TO DO LIST..

FOR TOMORROW..

NOTE..

DAILY PLAN

DATE

TODAY'S SCHEDULE

6-7 AM	
7-8 AM	
8-9 AM	
9-10 AM	
10-11 AM	
11-12 AM	
12-1 PM	
1-2 PM	
2-3 PM	
3-4 PM	
4-5 PM	
6-7 PM	
7-8 PM	
8-9 PM	

TOP PRIORITIES

TO DO LIST..

FOR TOMORROW..

NOTE..

DAILY PLAN

DATE

TODAY'S SCHEDULE

6-7 AM	
7-8 AM	
8-9 AM	
9-10 AM	
10-11 AM	
11-12 AM	
12-1 PM	
1-2 PM	
2-3 PM	
3-4 PM	
4-5 PM	
6-7 PM	
7-8 PM	
8-9 PM	

TOP PRIORITIES

FOR TOMORROW..

NOTE..

DAILY PLAN

TODAY'S SCHEDULE

6-7 AM	
7-8 AM	
8-9 AM	
9-10 AM	
10-11 AM	
11-12 AM	
12-1 PM	
1-2 PM	
2-3 PM	
3-4 PM	
4-5 PM	
6-7 PM	
7-8 PM	
8-9 PM	

TOP PRIORITIES

FOR TOMORROW..

NOTE..

DAILY PLAN

TODAY'S SCHEDULE

6-7 AM	
7-8 AM	
8-9 AM	
9-10 AM	
10-11 AM	
11-12 AM	
12-1 PM	
1-2 PM	
2-3 PM	
3-4 PM	
4-5 PM	
6-7 PM	
7-8 PM	
8-9 PM	

TOP PRIORITIES

NOTE..

DAILY PLAN

DATE

TODAY'S SCHEDULE

6-7 AM	
7-8 AM	
8-9 AM	
9-10 AM	
10-11 AM	
11-12 AM	
12-1 PM	
1-2 PM	
2-3 PM	
3-4 PM	
4-5 PM	
6-7 PM	
7-8 PM	
8-9 PM	

TOP PRIORITIES

TO DO LIST..

FOR TOMORROW..

NOTE..

DAILY PLAN

TODAY'S SCHEDULE

6-7 AM	
7-8 AM	
8-9 AM	
9-10 AM	
10-11 AM	
11-12 AM	
12-1 PM	
1-2 PM	
2-3 PM	
3-4 PM	
4-5 PM	
6-7 PM	
7-8 PM	
8-9 PM	

TOP PRIORITIES

TO DO LIST..

FOR TOMORROW..

NOTE..

DAILY PLAN

TODAY'S SCHEDULE

6-7 AM	
7-8 AM	
8-9 AM	
9-10 AM	
10-11 AM	
11-12 AM	
12-1 PM	
1-2 PM	
2-3 PM	
3-4 PM	
4-5 PM	
6-7 PM	
7-8 PM	
8-9 PM	

TOP PRIORITIES

NOTE..

DAILY PLAN

TODAY'S SCHEDULE

6-7 AM	
7-8 AM	
8-9 AM	
9-10 AM	
10-11 AM	
11-12 AM	
12-1 PM	
1-2 PM	
2-3 PM	
3-4 PM	
4-5 PM	
6-7 PM	
7-8 PM	
8-9 PM	

TOP PRIORITIES

TO DO LIST..

FOR TOMORROW..

NOTE..

DAILY PLAN

DATE

TODAY'S SCHEDULE

6-7 AM	
7-8 AM	
8-9 AM	
9-10 AM	
10-11 AM	
11-12 AM	
12-1 PM	
1-2 PM	
2-3 PM	
3-4 PM	
4-5 PM	
6-7 PM	
7-8 PM	
8-9 PM	

TOP PRIORITIES

TO DO LIST..

FOR TOMORROW..

NOTE..

DAILY PLAN

DATE

TODAY'S SCHEDULE

Time	
6-7 AM	
7-8 AM	
8-9 AM	
9-10 AM	
10-11 AM	
11-12 AM	
12-1 PM	
1-2 PM	
2-3 PM	
3-4 PM	
4-5 PM	
6-7 PM	
7-8 PM	
8-9 PM	

TOP PRIORITIES

TO DO LIST..

FOR TOMORROW..

NOTE..

DAILY PLAN

TODAY'S SCHEDULE

Time	
6-7 AM	
7-8 AM	
8-9 AM	
9-10 AM	
10-11 AM	
11-12 AM	
12-1 PM	
1-2 PM	
2-3 PM	
3-4 PM	
4-5 PM	
6-7 PM	
7-8 PM	
8-9 PM	

TOP PRIORITIES

TO DO LIST..

FOR TOMORROW..

NOTE..

DAILY PLAN

TODAY'S SCHEDULE

6-7 AM	
7-8 AM	
8-9 AM	
9-10 AM	
10-11 AM	
11-12 AM	
12-1 PM	
1-2 PM	
2-3 PM	
3-4 PM	
4-5 PM	
6-7 PM	
7-8 PM	
8-9 PM	

TOP PRIORITIES

NOTE..

DAILY PLAN

TODAY'S SCHEDULE

Time	
6-7 AM	
7-8 AM	
8-9 AM	
9-10 AM	
10-11 AM	
11-12 AM	
12-1 PM	
1-2 PM	
2-3 PM	
3-4 PM	
4-5 PM	
6-7 PM	
7-8 PM	
8-9 PM	

TOP PRIORITIES

NOTE..

DAILY PLAN

TODAY'S SCHEDULE

6-7 AM	
7-8 AM	
8-9 AM	
9-10 AM	
10-11 AM	
11-12 AM	
12-1 PM	
1-2 PM	
2-3 PM	
3-4 PM	
4-5 PM	
6-7 PM	
7-8 PM	
8-9 PM	

TOP PRIORITIES

NOTE..

DAILY PLAN

TODAY'S SCHEDULE

Time	
6-7 AM	
7-8 AM	
8-9 AM	
9-10 AM	
10-11 AM	
11-12 AM	
12-1 PM	
1-2 PM	
2-3 PM	
3-4 PM	
4-5 PM	
6-7 PM	
7-8 PM	
8-9 PM	

TOP PRIORITIES

FOR TOMORROW..

NOTE..

DAILY PLAN

DATE

TODAY'S SCHEDULE

Time	
6-7 AM	
7-8 AM	
8-9 AM	
9-10 AM	
10-11 AM	
11-12 AM	
12-1 PM	
1-2 PM	
2-3 PM	
3-4 PM	
4-5 PM	
6-7 PM	
7-8 PM	
8-9 PM	

TOP PRIORITIES

TO DO LIST..

FOR TOMORROW..

NOTE..

DAILY PLAN

DATE

TODAY'S SCHEDULE

6-7 AM	
7-8 AM	
8-9 AM	
9-10 AM	
10-11 AM	
11-12 AM	
12-1 PM	
1-2 PM	
2-3 PM	
3-4 PM	
4-5 PM	
6-7 PM	
7-8 PM	
8-9 PM	

TOP PRIORITIES

TO DO LIST..

FOR TOMORROW..

NOTE..

DAILY PLAN

TODAY'S SCHEDULE

6-7 AM	
7-8 AM	
8-9 AM	
9-10 AM	
10-11 AM	
11-12 AM	
12-1 PM	
1-2 PM	
2-3 PM	
3-4 PM	
4-5 PM	
6-7 PM	
7-8 PM	
8-9 PM	

TOP PRIORITIES

NOTE..

DAILY PLAN

TODAY'S SCHEDULE

6-7 AM	
7-8 AM	
8-9 AM	
9-10 AM	
10-11 AM	
11-12 AM	
12-1 PM	
1-2 PM	
2-3 PM	
3-4 PM	
4-5 PM	
6-7 PM	
7-8 PM	
8-9 PM	

TOP PRIORITIES

TO DO LIST..

FOR TOMORROW..

NOTE..

DAILY PLAN

TODAY'S SCHEDULE

6-7 AM	
7-8 AM	
8-9 AM	
9-10 AM	
10-11 AM	
11-12 AM	
12-1 PM	
1-2 PM	
2-3 PM	
3-4 PM	
4-5 PM	
6-7 PM	
7-8 PM	
8-9 PM	

TOP PRIORITIES

NOTE..

DAILY PLAN

DATE

TODAY'S SCHEDULE

6-7 AM	
7-8 AM	
8-9 AM	
9-10 AM	
10-11 AM	
11-12 AM	
12-1 PM	
1-2 PM	
2-3 PM	
3-4 PM	
4-5 PM	
6-7 PM	
7-8 PM	
8-9 PM	

TOP PRIORITIES

TO DO LIST..

FOR TOMORROW..

NOTE..

DAILY PLAN

TODAY'S SCHEDULE

6-7 AM	
7-8 AM	
8-9 AM	
9-10 AM	
10-11 AM	
11-12 AM	
12-1 PM	
1-2 PM	
2-3 PM	
3-4 PM	
4-5 PM	
6-7 PM	
7-8 PM	
8-9 PM	

TOP PRIORITIES

NOTE..

DAILY PLAN

TODAY'S SCHEDULE

6-7 AM	
7-8 AM	
8-9 AM	
9-10 AM	
10-11 AM	
11-12 AM	
12-1 PM	
1-2 PM	
2-3 PM	
3-4 PM	
4-5 PM	
6-7 PM	
7-8 PM	
8-9 PM	

TOP PRIORITIES

NOTE..

DAILY PLAN

TODAY'S SCHEDULE

6-7 AM	
7-8 AM	
8-9 AM	
9-10 AM	
10-11 AM	
11-12 AM	
12-1 PM	
1-2 PM	
2-3 PM	
3-4 PM	
4-5 PM	
6-7 PM	
7-8 PM	
8-9 PM	

TOP PRIORITIES

NOTE..

DAILY PLAN

DATE

TODAY'S SCHEDULE

6-7 AM	
7-8 AM	
8-9 AM	
9-10 AM	
10-11 AM	
11-12 AM	
12-1 PM	
1-2 PM	
2-3 PM	
3-4 PM	
4-5 PM	
6-7 PM	
7-8 PM	
8-9 PM	

TOP PRIORITIES

TO DO LIST..

FOR TOMORROW..

NOTE..

DAILY PLAN

TODAY'S SCHEDULE

6-7 AM	
7-8 AM	
8-9 AM	
9-10 AM	
10-11 AM	
11-12 AM	
12-1 PM	
1-2 PM	
2-3 PM	
3-4 PM	
4-5 PM	
6-7 PM	
7-8 PM	
8-9 PM	

TOP PRIORITIES

NOTE..

DAILY PLAN

TODAY'S SCHEDULE

6-7 AM	
7-8 AM	
8-9 AM	
9-10 AM	
10-11 AM	
11-12 AM	
12-1 PM	
1-2 PM	
2-3 PM	
3-4 PM	
4-5 PM	
6-7 PM	
7-8 PM	
8-9 PM	

TOP PRIORITIES

TO DO LIST..

FOR TOMORROW..

NOTE..

DAILY PLAN

TODAY'S SCHEDULE

6-7 AM	
7-8 AM	
8-9 AM	
9-10 AM	
10-11 AM	
11-12 AM	
12-1 PM	
1-2 PM	
2-3 PM	
3-4 PM	
4-5 PM	
6-7 PM	
7-8 PM	
8-9 PM	

TOP PRIORITIES

NOTE..

DAILY PLAN

TODAY'S SCHEDULE

6-7 AM	
7-8 AM	
8-9 AM	
9-10 AM	
10-11 AM	
11-12 AM	
12-1 PM	
1-2 PM	
2-3 PM	
3-4 PM	
4-5 PM	
6-7 PM	
7-8 PM	
8-9 PM	

TOP PRIORITIES

FOR TOMORROW..

NOTE..

DAILY PLAN

TODAY'S SCHEDULE

6-7 AM	
7-8 AM	
8-9 AM	
9-10 AM	
10-11 AM	
11-12 AM	
12-1 PM	
1-2 PM	
2-3 PM	
3-4 PM	
4-5 PM	
6-7 PM	
7-8 PM	
8-9 PM	

TOP PRIORITIES

NOTE..

DAILY PLAN

DATE

TODAY'S SCHEDULE

6-7 AM	
7-8 AM	
8-9 AM	
9-10 AM	
10-11 AM	
11-12 AM	
12-1 PM	
1-2 PM	
2-3 PM	
3-4 PM	
4-5 PM	
6-7 PM	
7-8 PM	
8-9 PM	

TOP PRIORITIES

TO DO LIST..

FOR TOMORROW..

NOTE..

DAILY PLAN

DATE

TODAY'S SCHEDULE

6-7 AM	
7-8 AM	
8-9 AM	
9-10 AM	
10-11 AM	
11-12 AM	
12-1 PM	
1-2 PM	
2-3 PM	
3-4 PM	
4-5 PM	
6-7 PM	
7-8 PM	
8-9 PM	

TOP PRIORITIES

TO DO LIST..

FOR TOMORROW..

NOTE..

DAILY PLAN

TODAY'S SCHEDULE

Time	
6-7 AM	
7-8 AM	
8-9 AM	
9-10 AM	
10-11 AM	
11-12 AM	
12-1 PM	
1-2 PM	
2-3 PM	
3-4 PM	
4-5 PM	
6-7 PM	
7-8 PM	
8-9 PM	

TOP PRIORITIES

TO DO LIST..

FOR TOMORROW..

NOTE..

DAILY PLAN

TODAY'S SCHEDULE

Time	
6-7 AM	
7-8 AM	
8-9 AM	
9-10 AM	
10-11 AM	
11-12 AM	
12-1 PM	
1-2 PM	
2-3 PM	
3-4 PM	
4-5 PM	
6-7 PM	
7-8 PM	
8-9 PM	

TOP PRIORITIES

NOTE..

DAILY PLAN

TODAY'S SCHEDULE

6-7 AM	
7-8 AM	
8-9 AM	
9-10 AM	
10-11 AM	
11-12 AM	
12-1 PM	
1-2 PM	
2-3 PM	
3-4 PM	
4-5 PM	
6-7 PM	
7-8 PM	
8-9 PM	

TOP PRIORITIES

NOTE..

DAILY PLAN

TODAY'S SCHEDULE

6-7 AM	
7-8 AM	
8-9 AM	
9-10 AM	
10-11 AM	
11-12 AM	
12-1 PM	
1-2 PM	
2-3 PM	
3-4 PM	
4-5 PM	
6-7 PM	
7-8 PM	
8-9 PM	

TOP PRIORITIES

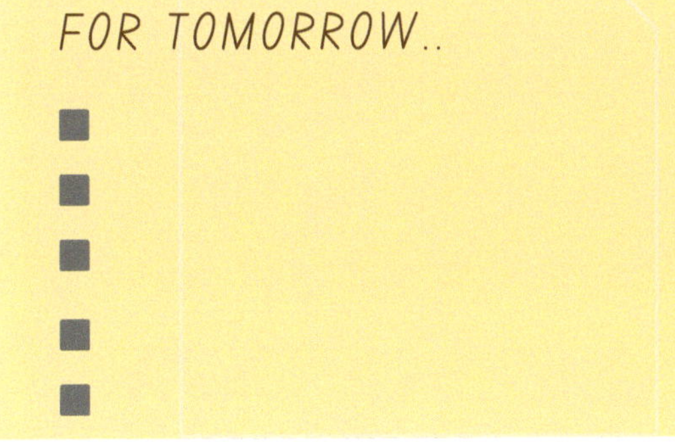

NOTE..

DAILY PLAN

TODAY'S SCHEDULE

Time	
6-7 AM	
7-8 AM	
8-9 AM	
9-10 AM	
10-11 AM	
11-12 AM	
12-1 PM	
1-2 PM	
2-3 PM	
3-4 PM	
4-5 PM	
6-7 PM	
7-8 PM	
8-9 PM	

TOP PRIORITIES

TO DO LIST..

FOR TOMORROW..

NOTE..

DAILY PLAN

DATE

TODAY'S SCHEDULE

Time	
6-7 AM	
7-8 AM	
8-9 AM	
9-10 AM	
10-11 AM	
11-12 AM	
12-1 PM	
1-2 PM	
2-3 PM	
3-4 PM	
4-5 PM	
6-7 PM	
7-8 PM	
8-9 PM	

TOP PRIORITIES

TO DO LIST..

FOR TOMORROW..

NOTE..

DAILY PLAN

TODAY'S SCHEDULE

Time	
6-7 AM	
7-8 AM	
8-9 AM	
9-10 AM	
10-11 AM	
11-12 AM	
12-1 PM	
1-2 PM	
2-3 PM	
3-4 PM	
4-5 PM	
6-7 PM	
7-8 PM	
8-9 PM	

TOP PRIORITIES

TO DO LIST..

FOR TOMORROW..

NOTE..

DAILY PLAN

TODAY'S SCHEDULE

6-7 AM	
7-8 AM	
8-9 AM	
9-10 AM	
10-11 AM	
11-12 AM	
12-1 PM	
1-2 PM	
2-3 PM	
3-4 PM	
4-5 PM	
6-7 PM	
7-8 PM	
8-9 PM	

TOP PRIORITIES

TO DO LIST..

FOR TOMORROW..

NOTE..

DAILY PLAN

TODAY'S SCHEDULE

6-7 AM	
7-8 AM	
8-9 AM	
9-10 AM	
10-11 AM	
11-12 AM	
12-1 PM	
1-2 PM	
2-3 PM	
3-4 PM	
4-5 PM	
6-7 PM	
7-8 PM	
8-9 PM	

TOP PRIORITIES

NOTE..

DAILY PLAN

DATE

TODAY'S SCHEDULE

6-7 AM	
7-8 AM	
8-9 AM	
9-10 AM	
10-11 AM	
11-12 AM	
12-1 PM	
1-2 PM	
2-3 PM	
3-4 PM	
4-5 PM	
6-7 PM	
7-8 PM	
8-9 PM	

TOP PRIORITIES

TO DO LIST..

FOR TOMORROW..

NOTE..

DAILY PLAN

TODAY'S SCHEDULE

Time	
6-7 AM	
7-8 AM	
8-9 AM	
9-10 AM	
10-11 AM	
11-12 AM	
12-1 PM	
1-2 PM	
2-3 PM	
3-4 PM	
4-5 PM	
6-7 PM	
7-8 PM	
8-9 PM	

TOP PRIORITIES

TO DO LIST..

FOR TOMORROW..

NOTE..

DAILY PLAN

TODAY'S SCHEDULE

Time	
6-7 AM	
7-8 AM	
8-9 AM	
9-10 AM	
10-11 AM	
11-12 AM	
12-1 PM	
1-2 PM	
2-3 PM	
3-4 PM	
4-5 PM	
6-7 PM	
7-8 PM	
8-9 PM	

TOP PRIORITIES

NOTE..

DAILY PLAN

TODAY'S SCHEDULE

6-7 AM	
7-8 AM	
8-9 AM	
9-10 AM	
10-11 AM	
11-12 AM	
12-1 PM	
1-2 PM	
2-3 PM	
3-4 PM	
4-5 PM	
6-7 PM	
7-8 PM	
8-9 PM	

TOP PRIORITIES

NOTE..

DAILY PLAN

TODAY'S SCHEDULE

6-7 AM	
7-8 AM	
8-9 AM	
9-10 AM	
10-11 AM	
11-12 AM	
12-1 PM	
1-2 PM	
2-3 PM	
3-4 PM	
4-5 PM	
6-7 PM	
7-8 PM	
8-9 PM	

TOP PRIORITIES

NOTE..

DAILY PLAN

TODAY'S SCHEDULE

6-7 AM	
7-8 AM	
8-9 AM	
9-10 AM	
10-11 AM	
11-12 AM	
12-1 PM	
1-2 PM	
2-3 PM	
3-4 PM	
4-5 PM	
6-7 PM	
7-8 PM	
8-9 PM	

TOP PRIORITIES

NOTE..

DAILY PLAN

DATE

TODAY'S SCHEDULE

6-7 AM	
7-8 AM	
8-9 AM	
9-10 AM	
10-11 AM	
11-12 AM	
12-1 PM	
1-2 PM	
2-3 PM	
3-4 PM	
4-5 PM	
6-7 PM	
7-8 PM	
8-9 PM	

TOP PRIORITIES

TO DO LIST..

FOR TOMORROW..

NOTE..

DAILY PLAN

DATE

TODAY'S SCHEDULE

6-7 AM	
7-8 AM	
8-9 AM	
9-10 AM	
10-11 AM	
11-12 AM	
12-1 PM	
1-2 PM	
2-3 PM	
3-4 PM	
4-5 PM	
6-7 PM	
7-8 PM	
8-9 PM	

TOP PRIORITIES

TO DO LIST..

FOR TOMORROW..

NOTE..

DAILY PLAN

TODAY'S SCHEDULE

6-7 AM	
7-8 AM	
8-9 AM	
9-10 AM	
10-11 AM	
11-12 AM	
12-1 PM	
1-2 PM	
2-3 PM	
3-4 PM	
4-5 PM	
6-7 PM	
7-8 PM	
8-9 PM	

TOP PRIORITIES

TO DO LIST..

FOR TOMORROW..

NOTE..

DAILY PLAN

TODAY'S SCHEDULE

Time
6-7 AM
7-8 AM
8-9 AM
9-10 AM
10-11 AM
11-12 AM
12-1 PM
1-2 PM
2-3 PM
3-4 PM
4-5 PM
6-7 PM
7-8 PM
8-9 PM

TOP PRIORITIES

TO DO LIST..

FOR TOMORROW..

NOTE..

DAILY PLAN

TODAY'S SCHEDULE

6-7 AM	
7-8 AM	
8-9 AM	
9-10 AM	
10-11 AM	
11-12 AM	
12-1 PM	
1-2 PM	
2-3 PM	
3-4 PM	
4-5 PM	
6-7 PM	
7-8 PM	
8-9 PM	

TOP PRIORITIES

NOTE..

DAILY PLAN

TODAY'S SCHEDULE

Time	
6-7 AM	
7-8 AM	
8-9 AM	
9-10 AM	
10-11 AM	
11-12 AM	
12-1 PM	
1-2 PM	
2-3 PM	
3-4 PM	
4-5 PM	
6-7 PM	
7-8 PM	
8-9 PM	

TOP PRIORITIES

NOTE..

DAILY PLAN

DATE

TODAY'S SCHEDULE

Time	
6-7 AM	
7-8 AM	
8-9 AM	
9-10 AM	
10-11 AM	
11-12 AM	
12-1 PM	
1-2 PM	
2-3 PM	
3-4 PM	
4-5 PM	
6-7 PM	
7-8 PM	
8-9 PM	

TOP PRIORITIES

TO DO LIST..

FOR TOMORROW..

NOTE..

DAILY PLAN

DATE

TODAY'S SCHEDULE

Time	
6-7 AM	
7-8 AM	
8-9 AM	
9-10 AM	
10-11 AM	
11-12 AM	
12-1 PM	
1-2 PM	
2-3 PM	
3-4 PM	
4-5 PM	
6-7 PM	
7-8 PM	
8-9 PM	

TOP PRIORITIES

TO DO LIST..

FOR TOMORROW..

NOTE..

DAILY PLAN

TODAY'S SCHEDULE

6-7 AM	
7-8 AM	
8-9 AM	
9-10 AM	
10-11 AM	
11-12 AM	
12-1 PM	
1-2 PM	
2-3 PM	
3-4 PM	
4-5 PM	
6-7 PM	
7-8 PM	
8-9 PM	

TOP PRIORITIES

TO DO LIST..

FOR TOMORROW..

NOTE..

DAILY PLAN

TODAY'S SCHEDULE

Time	
6-7 AM	
7-8 AM	
8-9 AM	
9-10 AM	
10-11 AM	
11-12 AM	
12-1 PM	
1-2 PM	
2-3 PM	
3-4 PM	
4-5 PM	
6-7 PM	
7-8 PM	
8-9 PM	

TOP PRIORITIES

NOTE..

DAILY PLAN

TODAY'S SCHEDULE

6-7 AM	
7-8 AM	
8-9 AM	
9-10 AM	
10-11 AM	
11-12 AM	
12-1 PM	
1-2 PM	
2-3 PM	
3-4 PM	
4-5 PM	
6-7 PM	
7-8 PM	
8-9 PM	

TOP PRIORITIES

TO DO LIST..

FOR TOMORROW..

NOTE..

DAILY PLAN

TODAY'S SCHEDULE

Time	
6-7 AM	
7-8 AM	
8-9 AM	
9-10 AM	
10-11 AM	
11-12 AM	
12-1 PM	
1-2 PM	
2-3 PM	
3-4 PM	
4-5 PM	
6-7 PM	
7-8 PM	
8-9 PM	

TOP PRIORITIES

NOTE..

DAILY PLAN

TODAY'S SCHEDULE

6-7 AM	
7-8 AM	
8-9 AM	
9-10 AM	
10-11 AM	
11-12 AM	
12-1 PM	
1-2 PM	
2-3 PM	
3-4 PM	
4-5 PM	
6-7 PM	
7-8 PM	
8-9 PM	

TOP PRIORITIES

NOTE..

DAILY PLAN

TODAY'S SCHEDULE

6-7 AM	
7-8 AM	
8-9 AM	
9-10 AM	
10-11 AM	
11-12 AM	
12-1 PM	
1-2 PM	
2-3 PM	
3-4 PM	
4-5 PM	
6-7 PM	
7-8 PM	
8-9 PM	

TOP PRIORITIES

TO DO LIST..

FOR TOMORROW..

NOTE..

DAILY PLAN

TODAY'S SCHEDULE

6-7 AM	
7-8 AM	
8-9 AM	
9-10 AM	
10-11 AM	
11-12 AM	
12-1 PM	
1-2 PM	
2-3 PM	
3-4 PM	
4-5 PM	
6-7 PM	
7-8 PM	
8-9 PM	

TOP PRIORITIES

TO DO LIST..

FOR TOMORROW..

NOTE..

DAILY PLAN

TODAY'S SCHEDULE

6-7 AM	
7-8 AM	
8-9 AM	
9-10 AM	
10-11 AM	
11-12 AM	
12-1 PM	
1-2 PM	
2-3 PM	
3-4 PM	
4-5 PM	
6-7 PM	
7-8 PM	
8-9 PM	

TOP PRIORITIES

TO DO LIST..

FOR TOMORROW..

NOTE..

DAILY PLAN

TODAY'S SCHEDULE

6-7 AM	
7-8 AM	
8-9 AM	
9-10 AM	
10-11 AM	
11-12 AM	
12-1 PM	
1-2 PM	
2-3 PM	
3-4 PM	
4-5 PM	
6-7 PM	
7-8 PM	
8-9 PM	

TOP PRIORITIES

NOTE..

DAILY PLAN

DATE

TODAY'S SCHEDULE

6-7 AM	
7-8 AM	
8-9 AM	
9-10 AM	
10-11 AM	
11-12 AM	
12-1 PM	
1-2 PM	
2-3 PM	
3-4 PM	
4-5 PM	
6-7 PM	
7-8 PM	
8-9 PM	

TOP PRIORITIES

TO DO LIST..

FOR TOMORROW..

NOTE..

DAILY PLAN

TODAY'S SCHEDULE

6-7 AM	
7-8 AM	
8-9 AM	
9-10 AM	
10-11 AM	
11-12 AM	
12-1 PM	
1-2 PM	
2-3 PM	
3-4 PM	
4-5 PM	
6-7 PM	
7-8 PM	
8-9 PM	

TOP PRIORITIES

TO DO LIST..

FOR TOMORROW..

NOTE..

DAILY PLAN

TODAY'S SCHEDULE

Time	
6-7 AM	
7-8 AM	
8-9 AM	
9-10 AM	
10-11 AM	
11-12 AM	
12-1 PM	
1-2 PM	
2-3 PM	
3-4 PM	
4-5 PM	
6-7 PM	
7-8 PM	
8-9 PM	

TOP PRIORITIES

TO DO LIST..

FOR TOMORROW..

NOTE..

DAILY PLAN

TODAY'S SCHEDULE

6-7 AM	
7-8 AM	
8-9 AM	
9-10 AM	
10-11 AM	
11-12 AM	
12-1 PM	
1-2 PM	
2-3 PM	
3-4 PM	
4-5 PM	
6-7 PM	
7-8 PM	
8-9 PM	

TOP PRIORITIES

TO DO LIST..

FOR TOMORROW..

NOTE..

DAILY PLAN

TODAY'S SCHEDULE

Time	
6-7 AM	
7-8 AM	
8-9 AM	
9-10 AM	
10-11 AM	
11-12 AM	
12-1 PM	
1-2 PM	
2-3 PM	
3-4 PM	
4-5 PM	
6-7 PM	
7-8 PM	
8-9 PM	

TOP PRIORITIES

NOTE..

DAILY PLAN

TODAY'S SCHEDULE

Time	
6-7 AM	
7-8 AM	
8-9 AM	
9-10 AM	
10-11 AM	
11-12 AM	
12-1 PM	
1-2 PM	
2-3 PM	
3-4 PM	
4-5 PM	
6-7 PM	
7-8 PM	
8-9 PM	

TOP PRIORITIES

NOTE..

DAILY PLAN

TODAY'S SCHEDULE

Time	
6-7 AM	
7-8 AM	
8-9 AM	
9-10 AM	
10-11 AM	
11-12 AM	
12-1 PM	
1-2 PM	
2-3 PM	
3-4 PM	
4-5 PM	
6-7 PM	
7-8 PM	
8-9 PM	

TOP PRIORITIES

TO DO LIST..

FOR TOMORROW..

NOTE..

DAILY PLAN

TODAY'S SCHEDULE

Time	
6-7 AM	
7-8 AM	
8-9 AM	
9-10 AM	
10-11 AM	
11-12 AM	
12-1 PM	
1-2 PM	
2-3 PM	
3-4 PM	
4-5 PM	
6-7 PM	
7-8 PM	
8-9 PM	

TOP PRIORITIES

NOTE..

DAILY PLAN

DATE

TODAY'S SCHEDULE

6-7 AM	
7-8 AM	
8-9 AM	
9-10 AM	
10-11 AM	
11-12 AM	
12-1 PM	
1-2 PM	
2-3 PM	
3-4 PM	
4-5 PM	
6-7 PM	
7-8 PM	
8-9 PM	

TOP PRIORITIES

TO DO LIST..

FOR TOMORROW..

NOTE..

DAILY PLAN

TODAY'S SCHEDULE

6-7 AM	
7-8 AM	
8-9 AM	
9-10 AM	
10-11 AM	
11-12 AM	
12-1 PM	
1-2 PM	
2-3 PM	
3-4 PM	
4-5 PM	
6-7 PM	
7-8 PM	
8-9 PM	

TOP PRIORITIES

NOTE..

DAILY PLAN

DATE

TODAY'S SCHEDULE

6-7 AM	
7-8 AM	
8-9 AM	
9-10 AM	
10-11 AM	
11-12 AM	
12-1 PM	
1-2 PM	
2-3 PM	
3-4 PM	
4-5 PM	
6-7 PM	
7-8 PM	
8-9 PM	

TOP PRIORITIES

TO DO LIST..

FOR TOMORROW..

NOTE..

DAILY PLAN

TODAY'S SCHEDULE

6-7 AM	
7-8 AM	
8-9 AM	
9-10 AM	
10-11 AM	
11-12 AM	
12-1 PM	
1-2 PM	
2-3 PM	
3-4 PM	
4-5 PM	
6-7 PM	
7-8 PM	
8-9 PM	

TOP PRIORITIES

NOTE..

DAILY PLAN

TODAY'S SCHEDULE

6-7 AM	
7-8 AM	
8-9 AM	
9-10 AM	
10-11 AM	
11-12 AM	
12-1 PM	
1-2 PM	
2-3 PM	
3-4 PM	
4-5 PM	
6-7 PM	
7-8 PM	
8-9 PM	

TOP PRIORITIES

NOTE..

DAILY PLAN

DATE

TODAY'S SCHEDULE

Time	
6-7 AM	
7-8 AM	
8-9 AM	
9-10 AM	
10-11 AM	
11-12 AM	
12-1 PM	
1-2 PM	
2-3 PM	
3-4 PM	
4-5 PM	
6-7 PM	
7-8 PM	
8-9 PM	

TOP PRIORITIES

TO DO LIST..

FOR TOMORROW..

NOTE..

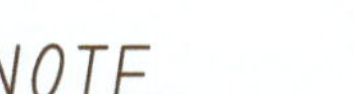

DAILY PLAN

TODAY'S SCHEDULE

6-7 AM	
7-8 AM	
8-9 AM	
9-10 AM	
10-11 AM	
11-12 AM	
12-1 PM	
1-2 PM	
2-3 PM	
3-4 PM	
4-5 PM	
6-7 PM	
7-8 PM	
8-9 PM	

TOP PRIORITIES

FOR TOMORROW..

NOTE..

DAILY PLAN

DATE

TODAY'S SCHEDULE

6-7 AM	
7-8 AM	
8-9 AM	
9-10 AM	
10-11 AM	
11-12 AM	
12-1 PM	
1-2 PM	
2-3 PM	
3-4 PM	
4-5 PM	
6-7 PM	
7-8 PM	
8-9 PM	

TOP PRIORITIES

TO DO LIST..

FOR TOMORROW..

NOTE..

DAILY PLAN

TODAY'S SCHEDULE

6-7 AM	
7-8 AM	
8-9 AM	
9-10 AM	
10-11 AM	
11-12 AM	
12-1 PM	
1-2 PM	
2-3 PM	
3-4 PM	
4-5 PM	
6-7 PM	
7-8 PM	
8-9 PM	

TOP PRIORITIES

FOR TOMORROW..

NOTE..

DAILY PLAN

TODAY'S SCHEDULE

6-7 AM	
7-8 AM	
8-9 AM	
9-10 AM	
10-11 AM	
11-12 AM	
12-1 PM	
1-2 PM	
2-3 PM	
3-4 PM	
4-5 PM	
6-7 PM	
7-8 PM	
8-9 PM	

TOP PRIORITIES

TO DO LIST..

FOR TOMORROW..

NOTE..

DAILY PLAN

TODAY'S SCHEDULE

6-7 AM	
7-8 AM	
8-9 AM	
9-10 AM	
10-11 AM	
11-12 AM	
12-1 PM	
1-2 PM	
2-3 PM	
3-4 PM	
4-5 PM	
6-7 PM	
7-8 PM	
8-9 PM	

TOP PRIORITIES

TO DO LIST..

FOR TOMORROW..

NOTE..

DAILY PLAN

TODAY'S SCHEDULE

6-7 AM	
7-8 AM	
8-9 AM	
9-10 AM	
10-11 AM	
11-12 AM	
12-1 PM	
1-2 PM	
2-3 PM	
3-4 PM	
4-5 PM	
6-7 PM	
7-8 PM	
8-9 PM	

TOP PRIORITIES

NOTE..

DAILY PLAN

TODAY'S SCHEDULE

6-7 AM	
7-8 AM	
8-9 AM	
9-10 AM	
10-11 AM	
11-12 AM	
12-1 PM	
1-2 PM	
2-3 PM	
3-4 PM	
4-5 PM	
6-7 PM	
7-8 PM	
8-9 PM	

TOP PRIORITIES

TO DO LIST..

FOR TOMORROW..

NOTE..

DAILY PLAN

TODAY'S SCHEDULE

6-7 AM	
7-8 AM	
8-9 AM	
9-10 AM	
10-11 AM	
11-12 AM	
12-1 PM	
1-2 PM	
2-3 PM	
3-4 PM	
4-5 PM	
6-7 PM	
7-8 PM	
8-9 PM	

TOP PRIORITIES

NOTE..

DAILY PLAN

DATE

TODAY'S SCHEDULE

6-7 AM	
7-8 AM	
8-9 AM	
9-10 AM	
10-11 AM	
11-12 AM	
12-1 PM	
1-2 PM	
2-3 PM	
3-4 PM	
4-5 PM	
6-7 PM	
7-8 PM	
8-9 PM	

TOP PRIORITIES

TO DO LIST..

FOR TOMORROW..

NOTE..

DAILY PLAN

TODAY'S SCHEDULE

Time	
6-7 AM	
7-8 AM	
8-9 AM	
9-10 AM	
10-11 AM	
11-12 AM	
12-1 PM	
1-2 PM	
2-3 PM	
3-4 PM	
4-5 PM	
6-7 PM	
7-8 PM	
8-9 PM	

TOP PRIORITIES

TO DO LIST..

FOR TOMORROW..

NOTE..

DAILY PLAN

DATE

TODAY'S SCHEDULE

6-7 AM	
7-8 AM	
8-9 AM	
9-10 AM	
10-11 AM	
11-12 AM	
12-1 PM	
1-2 PM	
2-3 PM	
3-4 PM	
4-5 PM	
6-7 PM	
7-8 PM	
8-9 PM	

TOP PRIORITIES

TO DO LIST..

FOR TOMORROW..

NOTE..

DAILY PLAN

DATE

TODAY'S SCHEDULE

6-7 AM	
7-8 AM	
8-9 AM	
9-10 AM	
10-11 AM	
11-12 AM	
12-1 PM	
1-2 PM	
2-3 PM	
3-4 PM	
4-5 PM	
6-7 PM	
7-8 PM	
8-9 PM	

TOP PRIORITIES

TO DO LIST..

FOR TOMORROW..

NOTE..

DAILY PLAN

DATE

TODAY'S SCHEDULE

Time	
6-7 AM	
7-8 AM	
8-9 AM	
9-10 AM	
10-11 AM	
11-12 AM	
12-1 PM	
1-2 PM	
2-3 PM	
3-4 PM	
4-5 PM	
6-7 PM	
7-8 PM	
8-9 PM	

TOP PRIORITIES

TO DO LIST..

FOR TOMORROW..

NOTE..

DAILY PLAN

TODAY'S SCHEDULE

6-7 AM	
7-8 AM	
8-9 AM	
9-10 AM	
10-11 AM	
11-12 AM	
12-1 PM	
1-2 PM	
2-3 PM	
3-4 PM	
4-5 PM	
6-7 PM	
7-8 PM	
8-9 PM	

TOP PRIORITIES

NOTE..

DAILY PLAN

TODAY'S SCHEDULE

6-7 AM	
7-8 AM	
8-9 AM	
9-10 AM	
10-11 AM	
11-12 AM	
12-1 PM	
1-2 PM	
2-3 PM	
3-4 PM	
4-5 PM	
6-7 PM	
7-8 PM	
8-9 PM	

TOP PRIORITIES

TO DO LIST..

FOR TOMORROW..

NOTE..

DAILY PLAN

DATE

TODAY'S SCHEDULE

6-7 AM	
7-8 AM	
8-9 AM	
9-10 AM	
10-11 AM	
11-12 AM	
12-1 PM	
1-2 PM	
2-3 PM	
3-4 PM	
4-5 PM	
6-7 PM	
7-8 PM	
8-9 PM	

TOP PRIORITIES

TO DO LIST..

FOR TOMORROW..

NOTE..

DAILY PLAN

TODAY'S SCHEDULE

Time	
6-7 AM	
7-8 AM	
8-9 AM	
9-10 AM	
10-11 AM	
11-12 AM	
12-1 PM	
1-2 PM	
2-3 PM	
3-4 PM	
4-5 PM	
6-7 PM	
7-8 PM	
8-9 PM	

TOP PRIORITIES

TO DO LIST..

FOR TOMORROW..

NOTE..